AIR FRYER RECIPES

Quick Cook Book

MAY 10, 2016

This document is geared towards providing exact and reliable information in regards to the topic and issue covered. The publication is sold with the idea that the publisher is not required to render accounting, officially permitted, or otherwise, qualified services. If advice is necessary, legal or professional, a practiced individual in the profession should be ordered.

- From a Declaration of Principles which was accepted and approved equally by a Committee of the American Bar Association and a Committee of Publishers and Associations.

The information provided herein is stated to be truthful and consistent, in that any liability, in terms of inattention or otherwise, by any usage or abuse of any policies, processes, or directions contained within is the solitary and utter responsibility of the recipient reader. Under no circumstances will any legal responsibility or blame be held against the publisher for any reparation, damages, or monetary loss due to the information herein, either directly or indirectly.

Baking and Frying demand as much time and is as much fun they seem to be. As the popular saying going, the difficult part about cooking food is the cooking part itself but airfryers have altered this situation at many homes. This is one such revolutionary product which has made the cooking process so much simpler and less time consuming. They aid us in the making of tasty and healthy food items in a shorter span of time.

Caution: Always grease the food items and the cooking grill before the airfryer machine is preheated.

Introduction

This book has been presented in an objective so as to provide a multi cuisine cooking experience to the reader. The recipes are simple and practical. The cooking time is also relatively less for these recipes as they are cooked with the help of an air fryer. This also is an added advantage that the calorie count and the fat content of the dishes are cut down into half of the actual numbers as airfryers do not consume much oil while cooking. The book is in simple language and the instructions are straight forward so the readers can follow the directions per se. The cuisines are as diverse as the recipes themselves. Few of them are local specialities of certain cuisines like the shewarmas, the tikkis and the muffins. The reader gets to know extra facts about the dish in addition to the recipe. Overall, the book aims at providing a comfortable at ease cooking experience for the reader.

Table of Contents

Chapter 1

Starters

Table of Contents

Matar Potato Kebab

Potato Wedges

Ingredients.....................Quantity

Potatoes...3-5

Turmeric Powder................................1 tsp

Red Chilli Powder..............................2 tsp

Dry Mango Powder.............................1 tsp

Preparation

1. Marinate the potatoes with the mixture of Turmeric Powder, Red Chilli Powder and dry mango powder in appropriate amounts (This can be decided if the person likes the wedges to be spicier or less spicy).

2. Sprinkle salt over the potatoes which are marinated. Mix them well so that the salt is spread to the wedges evenly.

3. Preheat the Airfryer for 3 minutes on 180*C (355*F).

4. Brush the wedges a little oil and cook them at the same temperature for about 15 minutes.

Extra Facts

In case of cheese potato wedges, grate cheese cubes and sprinkle the cheese over the marinated potatoes before baking them.

Spring Rolls

Ingredients.....................Quantity

Stalk Onion (Large)........................... 1

Corn Oil...2 tbsp

Ginger, Garlic (Minced)................... 2

Chicken Fillet (Minced)................... 2

Mushrooms (Diced)....................... 10

Mixed Spices (your choice)............. 2 tsp

Cabbage (Minced)........................... 4 cups

Salt..1 teaspoon

Black Pepper....................................¼ tsp

Tomato Paste....................................2 tbsp

Corn starch ....1 tbsp

Soya Sauce.......................................3 tbsp

Vinegar...2 tbsp

Chinese Spring rolls.......................1 packet

Preparation

1. In a pan, fry the onion with ginger and garlic. As the onion turns transparent, add the chicken, mushrooms and cabbage. Let the chicken cook well as u add the spices with salt and black pepper.

2. In another bowl, add the tomato paste with the soya sauce, corn starch with water and make it a semi paste. Now

add the chicken to the paste and let it settle.

3. Mix the previous mixture with the semi paste. This will make the filling for the spring roll.

4. Stuff the filling into the spring rolls and adjust the edges from leaking the filling with the help of egg white.

5. Spread oil in a butter paper and the rolls are spread with oil.

6. Preheat the Air Fryer at 180*C (355*F) and let it cook for 10 minutes.

Extra Facts

The spring rolls can be served with tomato ketchup or with mint mayonnaise.

French Fries with Meat Sauce

Ingredients......................Quantity

Onion (Minced, Large)........................1

Garlic, Cloves (Minced).................... 1

Corn Oil...2 tbsp

Meat (Minced)............................. 7 oz (200 g)

Tomato (Large, Peeled & Minced).... 2

Salt...1 tsp

Black Pepper......................................1 tsp

Corriander (Dried)............................ 1 tsp

Potato Fingers (Fried)...................... 4 packets

Cheese (Shredded)........................... ½ cup

Preparation

1. Heat oil, add onion, garlic and pepper. Mix the meat and let the mixture dry.

2. Add the tomatoes with the salt, cumin and coriander, cook on low heat for 10 minutes.

3. Place the potato fingers in a plate, sprinkle cheese in abundance or less as required. Add the meat mix to the fries and leave it in the Air Fryer for 5 minutes at 180*C (355*F).

Extra Facts

Serve the French fries with spicy pickles to match the meat.

Cottage Cheese Sticks

Ingredients......................Quantity

Paneer..7 oz (200 g)

Lemon (Juiced)................................. 1

Ginger- Garlic (Paste)........................ 2 tbsp

Salt...1 tsp

Red Chilli Powder..............................1 tsp

Corn Flour...5 tbsp

Water...1 cup

Preparation

1. Cut the cottage cheese into long pieces.

2. With the lemon juice, garlic-ginger paste, salt and red chilli powder, make a paste.

3. Dip the paneer in the paste and marinate it for a while.

4. Roll the paneer in corn flour. Let it settle for about 20 minutes.

5. Pre heat the Air Fryer for 5 minutes at 160*C (320*F). Maintain the heat to be 160*C (320*F) as we roll the paneer to cook uniformly.

Extra Facts

Use Tomato Ketchup or Mayonnaise as the dip for the dish.

Garnish it with shredded cheese to make the dish more cheesy.

Chicken Croquettes

Ingredients.....................Quantity

Chicken (with bones.................. 1 ½ lb (600 g)

Garlic (Crushed)......................................½ tsp

Water..½ cup

Butter..2 tbsp

Flour...6 tbsp

Mushrooms (Chopped)...........................5

Onions (Chopped)............................... ½ cup

Parsley...1 tbsp

White Pepper.......................................½ tbsp

Chilli Flakes..½ tbsp

Cheese (Grated)......................... 1 ½ oz (40 g)

Jalapenos...1 tbsp

Kernels..½ tbsp

Bread Slice (Crumbled)...................... ½ cup

Preparation

1. Mix the chicken with water to boil and add the garlic to the pressure cooker.

2. Let it cook on high flame and let the pressure drop. Shred the chicken into fine pieces and discard the bones from the chicken.

3. Add butter to a pan, add the flour and stir on low flame for ½ minute. Add boiled chicken and stir for 1 minute.

4. Add parsley, salt, white pepper, red chilli flakes, corn, jalapenos/green chillies, ½ cup fresh bread crumbs and cheese.

5. Roll them and on a flat surface to make uniform croquettes.

For batter

6. Mix bread crumbs with salt and parsley. Dip in egg white. Again roll over corn flour and then dip in egg white. The rolls are then applied with bread crumbs.

7. Pre heat the Oxy Fryer at 160*C (320*F) for 5 minutes. To cook uniformly turn the croquettes every now and then.

Extra Facts

You can Serve hot with tomato sauce/cheesedip.

Chicken Wings

Ingredients......................Quantity

Chicken Wings....................................12

Ginger Garlic paste............................1 tbsp

Soya Sauce...1 tbsp

Vinegar..2 tsp

Pepper...½ tsp

Dry red Chillies.................................2

Water..1 cup

For batter

Egg Whites 2

Flour...2 tbsp

Corn Flour...A Pinch

Salt..½ tsp

Pepper...1 tbsp

Tomato Ketchup...............................1 tbsp

Vinegar...1 tbsp

Preparation

1. The red chillies are grinded with the ginger-garlic paste. The soya sauce is

then added with the paste along with pepper, salt and oil.

2. The chicken wings are marinated and left in the refrigerator for 2 to 3 hours.

3. The batter is mixed well to avoid lumps.

4. Pre heat the Oxy Fryer for 5 minutes at 160*C (320*F).

5. The wings are dipped in the batter and kept aside. The wings are mixed in the batter and fried in the oxy fryer.

6. The fryer is maintained at 160*C (320*F) for 12-15 minutes.

Extra Facts

Ketchup , Vinegar, Soya Sauce and Pepper are optional seasoning for better taste. Chilli Sauce can also be served with the wings.

Tiger Prawn Crispy Lollipop

Ingredients.....................Quantity

Jumbo Prawns -

(De veined and Cleaned).....................6 pieces

Bamboo Sticks...10

Lemon Juice...1 cup

Marinade

Garlic Paste...2 tsp

Salt...½ teaspoon

Ginger Paste...2 tsp

For Batter

Yoghurt (Plain)..................................... ½ cups

Flour.....................................1 cup

Pepper.....................................1 cup

Baking powder.....................................½ cup

Turmeric...½ tbsp

Baking Powder.....................................1 tbsp

Mint(Chopped).................................. 4 tbsp

Coriander...1 cup

Salt ....½ tbsp

Coating

Crushed Cornflakes..............................½ cup

Chilli Flakes..½ tsp

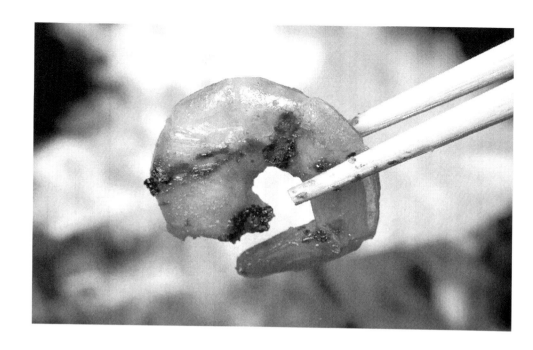

Preparation

1. The prawns are sprinkled with lemon juice and kept aside for 15 minutes.

2. The ingredients of the marinade are mixed well and kept in a bowl. The prawns are mixed with the marinade and kept aside for half an hour.

3. The prawns are added to the bamboo sticks. They are covered with the cornflakes mixture. This mixture is refrigerated about 15 minutes.

4. The Air Fryer is pre heated for 10 minutes at 160*C (320*F) and are allowed to cook.

5. Care has to be taken so that the prawns are cooked uniformly.

Extra Facts

We can sprinkle a little chaat masala and serve this with Puthina Chutney.

Chicken Tikki

Ingredients......................Quantity

Chicken-

(Boneless cut into pieces)............ 1 lb (500 g)

Chaat Masala...1 tsp

Lemon Juice..½ cup

Marinade

Vinegar..2 tbsp

Pepper...½ tsp

Ginger-Garlic Paste...............................2 tsp

Tandoori Masala....................................2 tbsp

Black Salt..½ tsp

Red Chilli Powder.................................½ cup

Preparation

1. Cut the chicken breast into two pieces from the middle. Cut the chicken in the shape of fingers and pat them dry with a towel.

2. Mix all the ingredients for marinade and add the chicken slices to the marinade. Keep it aside for about an hour or two.

3. Mix oregano and chilli flakes with the bread crumbs. Roll the marinated chicken over the breadcrumb mixture. Refrigerate it for about an hour.

4. Pre Heat the Air Fryer at 160*C (320*F) for 5 minutes. Cook the chicken for 15 minutes at 140*C (285*F) and make sure the chicken is cooked uniformly.

Extra Facts

Serve with green chutney or mint mayonnaise.

Vegetable and Oats Muffins

Ingredients.....................Quantity

Whole Wheat Flour.............................¾ cup

Salt...2 tsp

Oregano...1 tbsp

Dry basil..½ tsp

Baking Powder....................................½ tsp

Baking Soda...¼ tsp

Curd...½ cup

Milk...½ cup

Mixed Vegetables (Chopped) ....½ cup

Preparation

1. Mix the flour, oats with the baking powder and baking soda.

2. Add salt, basil and oregano with the salt. Beat the curd until it turns smooth.

3. The potatoes are boiled until they are cooked. Add oil to this and mix to coat.

4. Add flour and vegetables to mix. Add milk to get the best consistency.

5. Empty the batter in silver muffin cups and top them with nuts or anything of your choice.

6. Pre heat the air fryer at 160*C (320*F) for about 5 minutes.

7. Let it bake at the same temperature for 20 to 25 minutes.

Extra Facts

Serve them with tomato ketchup.

Chilli Paneer

Ingredients.....................Quantity

Cottage Cheese...........................5 ¼ oz (150g)

Capsicum (Big, cut into cubes).............1

Red Onion (Small)...............................1

Spring Onion...1

Marinate

Ginger-Garlic Paste................................1 tbsp

Red chilli sauce..1 tbsp

Salt...2 tsp

Pepper...2 tsp

Coating

Corn Flour...3 tbsp

Gravy

Green chillies (Finely Chopped)............. 1-2

Ginger... ½ tsp

Garlic (Chopped).................................... 1 tsp

Tomato Ketchup.....................................3 tbsp

Vinegar..2 tsp

Soya Sauce..2 tsp

Water..1 cup

Olive Oil...1 tbsp

Preparation

1. Cut the cottage cheese pieces so that they remain attached to one another.

2. Mix the marinade ingredients together and make it as a paste. Apply the marinade paste uniformly over the cottage cheese.

3. Roll the cheese with the corn flour.

4. Pre heat the Air Fryer for 5 minutes at 180*C (355*F).

5. Cook the pieces for 20 minutes at the same temperature about another 20 minutes. Turn the pieces as they cook so that they are fried uniformly.

6. Prepare the gravy by heating the olive oil with garlic, green chillies and ginger. Add some onions and saute them for 2 minutes. Cook this with the ginger garlic paste and fry till the mixture is softened by cooking.

7. Add the sauce mixture and let the mixture boil for some time. The water and corn flour mix is then added to it.

8. Add cheese and green onions. Cook them and the sauce is let to settle over the cottage cheese.

Extra Facts

The Cottage Cheese can be served with green chutney.

Mushroom Tikka

Ingredients.....................Quantity

Mushrooms...................................3.5 oz (100g)

Cinnamon Stick...................................1 piece

Cardamom...2

Cloves...2-3

Black Peppercorns.............................6

Salt...½ tsp

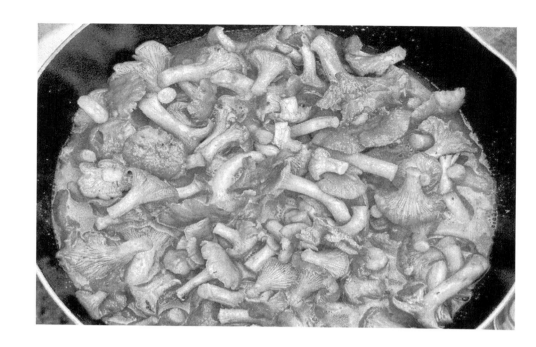

Preparation

1. Boil the water with the spices and salt. As the water starts boiling, the mushrooms are added.

2. Boil the mushrooms for about 3 to 4 minutes.

3. Mix the yoghurt, ginger garlic paste, red chilli powder, garam masala, tandoori masala and mint leaves.

4. Add few drops of lemon juice to the mixture and add corn flour to this.

5. Pre heat the airfryer for 5 minutes at 160*C (320*F).

6. Arrange it in the fry basket and close it. Let it fry at 160*C (320*F) for another 20 minutes. Turn the mushrooms so that they are uniformly cooked.

7. Add a few drops of lemon juice as the mixture cools down at room temperature.

Extra Facts

The dish is best served with green chutney.

Crispy Garlic Potato Fingers

Ingredients....................Quantity

Potatoes (Peeled, Big)........................... 2

Ginger- Garlic Paste...............................2 tsp

Red Chilli Sauce....................................1 tbsp

Red Chilli Powder.................................¼ tsp

Black Pepper...¼ tsp

Preparation

1. In a bowl, mix the ginger-garlic paste with the red chilli sauce along with pepper and salt.

2. Boil the water with salt and potato fingers are boiled along for 5 minutes.

3. Filter and dry the potatoes with a dry towel.

4. Coat the potatoes with the sauce mixture.

5. Pre heat the Air fryer at 160*C for about 5 minutes.

6. Keep the potatoes in the fry basket and let it cook for 20 minutes.

7. Toss the potatoes through the cooking so that they are fried uniformly.

Extra Facts

Serve them with main courses as starters with dips and tomato ketchup.

Masala French Fries

Ingredients......................Quantity

Potatoes (Peeled, Medium, Cut)....... 3

Marinate

Olive Oil...2 tbsp
Mixed Herbs..2 tbsp
Red Chilli Flakes................................¼ tbsp
Salt...½ tbsp
Lemon Juice.......................................1 tabsp

Garnishing

Coriander (Finely Chopped)............. 2 tbsp

Preparation

1. The marinate ingredients are mixed together.

2. Boil the water with salt and blanch the potatoes.

3. Coat the potatoes with the mixture and let it set in the potatoes.

4. Pre heat the Air Fryer at 180*C (355*F) for 5 minutes.

5. Put the potatoes in the fry basket.

6. Fry the potatoes at 150*C (300*F) for about 25-30 minutes.

7. Toss the potatoes to cook uniformly.

8. Let the potatoes cool down, sprinkle the corianders which are chopped.

Extra Facts

This can be served with mayonnaise or any dip.

Crispy Dhingri Kebab

Ingredients.....................Quantity

Mushrooms (Boiled, Large)............... 5

Dal (Channa)....................................... ½ cup

Ginger (Grated).................................... ½ cup

Green Chillies.......................................2-3

Red Chilli Powder................................½ tsp

Salt...1 tsp

Coriander Powder...............................½ tsp

Coriander (Chopped)......................... 2 tbsp

Bread Crumbs......................................1 cup

Lemon Juice...1 tsp

Preparation

1. Boil the daal in a vessel until it is cooked. Care should be taken that it does not turn soggy.

2. Grind the daal with the ginger and green chillies to form a thick paste. Pour some water in case of necessity.

3. Bread crumps and the masala is mixed together along with the mushrooms.

4. Mix well so that the dough becomes soft enough to be stuffed inside the mushrooms.

5. Wet the mushrooms with little milk and the dough is rolled inside the mushrooms.

6. Pre heat the Air Fryer at 200*C (390*F) for about 5 minutes. Fry the mushrooms in the fry basket.

7. Cook the mushrooms for about 30 minutes at the same temperature.

8. Turn the kebabs as they cook uniformly.

9. Serve hot.

Extra Facts

Serve them with green chutney or
mayonnaise.

Matar Potato Kebab

Ingredients.....................Quantity

Peas (Boiled)... 1 cup

Chicken(Boiled, Small)............... 3.5 oz (100g)

Chillies (Green, Chopped)................... 2

Cashews..10-12

Salt...To taste

Pepper...To taste

Ginger (Grated)................................. ½ tsp

Elachi Powder......................................3 pinch

Chaat Masala..................................To Sprinkle

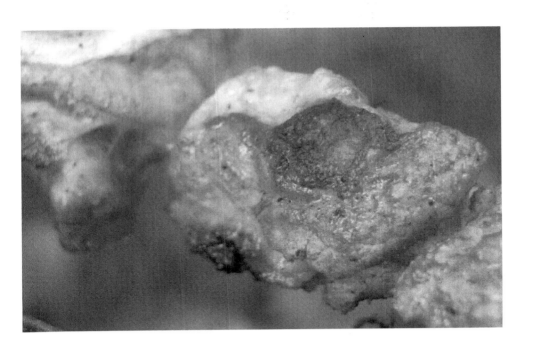

Preparation

1. Roast the Cashews with the chicken.

2. Dry roast the peas for about 3 minutes. now grind the peas, ginger and green chillies to form a paste.

3. Mix the chicken and the cashew powder with the peas paste.

4. Add required amount of salt, masala and pepper to this.

5. Mix them well so that they can formed in the shape of skewers or kebabs.

6. Pre heat the Air Fryer for about 5 minutes at 200*C (390*F).

7. Arrange the kebabs in the fryer basket.

8. Keep turning the kebabs till they are cooked completely.

9. Remove them when they are done. Let them cool down to room temperature.

Extra Facts

The kebabs can be served with chutney and lemon can be sprinkled over them.

Chapter 2

Main
Courses

Table of Contents

Chicken Shawerma

Ingredients..................Quantity

Butter...2 tbsp

Chicken (Cut into thin strips)...... 10 oz (300g)

Onion (Large)...................................... 1

Garlic, Cloves (Sliced)......................... 2-3

Vinegar..½ Cup

Cream..250 ml

Salt...1 tsp

Black Pepper.......................................½ tsp

Flat Bread...1 packet

Tomato (Medium)............................. 1

Pickles- (optional)...............................1 tsp

Preparation

1. Heat Butter in a pan and add the chicken strips to the butter. Stir until the chicken turns golden in colour.

2. Add onion, garlic to the meat and let it fry until the onions become transparent.

3. Add vinegar to the mixture and a spoon of cream to it till it turns saucy.

4. Finally add few chopped tomatoes to this and let the mixture settle down.

5. Now, the mixture can be rolled in the flat bread and is cooked in the airfryer preheated at 200*C.

6. Arrange the dish in a plate and serve it with pickles.

7. Garnish with lettuces.

Extra Facts

Shawarma is a popular Arabic Meat preparation which can be served as a quick snack to a full fledged meal. It can be dressed using spices and spicy sauces.

Mutton Cream Tart

Ingredients......................Quantity

Pastry Puff Squares............................1 packet
Egg (Beaten)...................................... 1

For Filling

Cumin Seeds..1 tsp
Butter...2 tbsp
Mutton (Chopped)..................... 8 ¾ oz (250g)
Onions (Medium)............................... 1
Salt...1 tsp
Black Pepper......................................½ tsp
Oregano (Dried).............................. ½ tsp
Basil...¼ tsp
Cheese (Crumbled)........................... ½ cup

Preparation

1. Arrange the pastry squares and spread butter evenly over the squares.

2. For the filling: Fry the cumin seeds along with the meat and other ingredients.

3. Add salt to the filling mixture.

4. Cook well under medium flame and add the cream to the mixture.

5. Spoon the filling evenly over the pastry squares and sprinkle required amount of cheese over the stuffed pastry squares.

6. Bake the filled squares for about 15 minutes.

7. Serve hot with mayonnaise dip.

Extra Facts

One can add anything to the filling according to your taste preferences.

Meat Loaf

Ingredients.....................Quantity

Meat (Finely Minced)................ 1 ½ lbs (750g)

Tomato Paste......................................1 Packet

Parsley...½ cup

Breadcrumps.......................................½ cup

Egg..1

Salt...2 tsp

Black pepper.......................................1 tsp

Paprika...1 tsp

Chilli..1 tsp

Preparation

1. In a bowl, add meat with tomato paste, parsley, breadcrumbs, egg, salt, pepper, paprika, chilli and spices. Mix with fingers softly.

2. Pre heat the Air fryer at 170*C (340*F) and cook the meat for about 50 to 60 minutes.

3. Along with the cooked meat, spread the tomato paste and let it cool for about 5 minutes.

4. Serve with bread or rice or vegetables along with the meat loaf.

Extra Facts

Garnish with onions and coriander. Pour lemon juice over the meat to acquire a better flavour.

Potatoes and Beef Casserole

Ingredients.....................Quantity

Potatoes (Large, Peeled).....................4

Butter..2 tbsp

Onion (Medium, Chopped).................1

Cloves, Garlic (Minced).......................2

Thick Cream....................................250 ml pack

Salt..2 tbsp

White Pepper.....................................¼ tsp

Bread Crumples................................2 tbsp

For Filling

Butter..2 tbsp

Beef...8 ¾ oz (250g)

Onion (Chopped, Medium)..................1

Garlic (Minced).....................................2

Tomato Paste......................................2 tbsp

Cumin..1

Turmeric Powder...............................½ tbsp

Preparation

1. Filling: Cook the beef with butter until it's dry and add onions, tomato paste. Add salt to the mixture.

2. Boil the potatoes in water and add salt, simmer for about 10-15 minutes.

3. Saute the onions and garlic for about 5 minutes.

4. Mash the potatoes and add cream to the mashed potatoes. Add the fried onion to the mashed potatoes.

5. Place half of the potatoes in the Air Fryer and the filling should be spread over the layer of mashed potatoes. The filling is again covered with mashed potatoes.

6. Bake the mix in the Air Fryer for about 15-20 minutes until it turns brown in colour.

Extra Facts

The beef meat can be replaced with any other meat. The garnishing can be further done with extra vegetables.

Fish with Tomato Sauce

Ingredients....................Quantity

Fish Fillet...4 pieces

Flour...cup

Salt..2 tsp

Black pepper...1 tsp

Fish Spices..2 tsp

Oil...1 cup

Onion (Large).......................................1

Garlic (Minced)....................................1

Coriander (Chopped)........................ 1 cup

Tomato Paste....................................4 tbsp

Cumin...1 tsp

Lomy...2 pieces

Lemon juice......................................2 tbsp

Preparation

1. Put the flour in a bowl, add a little salt, pepper and the fish spices. Cover the fillets with the flour with the mixes.

2. Add the tomato paste to sauted onions (in a separate pan) with coriander. To the paste add the lomy, lemon juice and the cumin.

3. Pour the sauce over the fish and cook it in the Air Fryer at 180*C (355*F) for about 15-20 minutes.

Extra Facts

Garnish with spring onions and coriander.

Burritos

Ingredients.....................Quantity

Refried beans...1 cup

Red Kidney Beans (Soak overnight)... 1 cup

Onion (Medium, Chopped)................. 1

Olive Oil...2 tsp

Tomato Paste...4 tbsp

Salt...2 tsp

Flour Tortillas...4-5

For Filling

Olive oil..2 tbsp

Onion (Sliced)... 1

Garlic (Crushed)................................... 6

Mushrooms..............................3 ½ oz (100 g)

Paneer (Cottage Cheese)........... 3 ½ oz (100 g)

Cabbage (Finely Shredded)................... ½ cup

Vinegar...1 tbsp

Salt...1 tbsp

Carrots (Chopped).............................. 2 tbsp

Preparation

1. Boil the beans and mash them well. Add chopped onion and garlic with the mashed beans.

2. Fry the onions with the tomato paste, now add the mashed beans with salt and red chilli. Let the paste boil and become a semi liquid puree.

3. Heat oil in a pan. Cook onions and mushrooms(Optional) and stir for about 10 minutes. As the last step, add cottage cheese and cabbage with the onions. To lubricate the mixture add vinegar, chilli flakes with pepper.

4. Spread the tortillas and fill them with the beans paste and the other fillings.

5. Pre heat the Air Fryer for 5 minutes at 200*C (390*F). Cook for about 200*C (390*F) for 15-20 minutes. Turn the burritos mid way for them to fry uniformly.

Extra Facts

We can also add shredded cheese with the burritos.

They can also be served with salads in case of serving them as the main dish.

Fish Pot Pie

Ingredients......................Quantity

Frozen Puff Pastry............................1 sheet
Egg (Large, Beaten)........................... 1

For Filling

Butter..4 tbsp
Onion (Medium, Chopped)................ 1
Milk..2 cups
Bay Leaves..2
Salt...1 tsp
Oregano (Dried)................................ 1 tsp
Fish Fillet...................................14 oz (400 g)
Flour..½ cup
Carrot..1
Cream...250 ml

Mozarella Cheese...............................1 cup

Preparation

1. Preheat the Air Fryer at 180*C (355*F).

2. In a pan, melt the butter and add onions to cook until they turn transparent, add milk, bay leaves, salt, pepper and oregano to cook.

3. Add the fish fillets along with the carrots. The fish is cooked until it turns tender.

4. In another pan, add the butter, flour and cook well for 2 minutes. Add milk and cream to the mixture. Make this as a thick sauce.

5. Fill the sauce to the fish, sprinkle the mozzarella cheese over it.

6. Roll the filling and fill it as strips and brush it with egg.

7. Bake the strips for about 25-30 minutes in the Air Fryer.

Extra Facts

The filling can be changed as per taste. The fillings can be chicken or mutton also.

Baked Fish in Curry Bechamal

Ingredients.....................Quantity

Boneless Fish..............................10 oz (300 g)

Lemon Juice...............................1 tbsp

Milk...½ cup

Onion (Finely Chopped)......................1

Carrot (Small)................................1

Bay Leaf......................................1

Butter..4 tbsp

Flour..2 tbsp

Water..1 cup

Pepper.......................................½ tsp

Sugar...½ tsp

Curry Powder...............................2 tsp

Preparation

1. Rub lemon juice over the fish and let the juice set into the fish.

2. Boil the milk with onions, carrots and a bay leaf. Remove from flame.

3. Add flour to the butter and stir the colour is changed.

4. The milk and butter with the flour are mixed together.

5. The sauce should thicken and add pepper, sugar and the vegetables with the curry powder.

6. Add required amount of salt and the bay leaf is removed.

7. The Oxy Fryer is heated for 5 minutes and the fish is cooked at 160*C (320*F) for about 5 minutes. Let the fish cook uniformly. Turn the fish as it cooks in the Air Fryer.

Extra Facts

This can be served as the main dish or a starter depending upon the quantity and the taste preferences.

Beef with Creamy Sauce

Ingredients.....................Quantity

Beef (Boneless)......................... 2 ¼ lb (1 kg)

Butter...2-3 tsp

Onion (Medium, Chopped)................. 2-3

Garlic (Minced, Chopped).................. 1 tsp

Mixed spices.....................................1 tsp

Salt..2 tsp

Black Pepper......................................1 tsp

Tomato Paste....................................250 ml

Potatoes (Cubed) 2

Carrots...2

Cream ....250 ml

Flat Bread...1packet

Coriander...1 cup

Preparation

1. Cut the beef into cube pieces.

2. Add butter and onion, fry them till the onions turn transparent.

3. Add the beef cubes and stir they turn brown. Add coriander, Cumin, spices, salt and pepper. Add tomato paste to the

mixture. Add Potatoes, Carrots and chillies.

4. Cook the mixture for 20-25 minutes at 180*C (355*F).

5. Sprinkle coriander over the cooked food and serve hot.

Extra Facts

Apply sauce on top as an add on.

Lamb Shank

Ingredients....................Quantity

Lamb Shanks.....................................4 pieces

Mixed Spices...½ tsp

Salt..½ tsp

Cinnamon...½ tsp

Cardamom..½ tsp

Onion (Large, Chopped)......................1

Cloves, Garlic (Minced)......................4

Carrot (Chopped)................................ 1

Mushrooms (Chopped).......................8

Tomatoes (Peeled and Minced)............2

Oregano ....½ tsp

Tomato Paste.......................................5 tbsp

Preparation

1. Place the mutton in a plate and sprinkle the spices, cumin, cardamom and other spices.

2. Heat oil and fry the mutton with onion, garlic, ginger and mushrooms.

3. Add the carrots and oregano with the tomato paste and pre heat the air fryer at 180*C (355*F) for about 10 minutes.

4. Cook the dish at 180*C (355*F) for another 20 minutes.

Extra Facts

Add grated vegetables of your choice over the dish.

Baked Penne Pasta

Ingredients......................Quantity

Pasta...1 cup

Boiling Water....................................5-6 cups

Olive...1 tbsp

Capsicums..3

Carrot (Small)....................................2

Salt ....1 tsp

Pepper..1 tsp

Oregano (Dried)................................½ cup

Preparation

1. Boil 5 to 6 cups of water. Add salt to the water and little drops of water.

2. The pasta is boiled in the water and is cooked till it turns soft.

3. Saute the carrtos for about 2-3 minutes. Cook with capsicum with this mixture.

4. Add required amount of salt and pepper.

5. For white sauce

6. Boil milk with basil leaves and strain the basil leaves. The olive oil is heated in a pan. The flour is added and stirred for about a minute.

7. Keep adding the milk until the paste becomes thick in consistency. The salt and pepper are added to the mixture.

8. Coat the pasta with the sauce and sprinkle a little amount of grated cheese.

9. Pre heat the Air Fryer for about 5 minutes at 160*C (320*F). Cook the pasta for about 10 to 12 minutes at the same temperature.

10.   Stir the pasta to cook uniformly.

Extra Facts

Grated Cheese can be sprinkled over the dish.
Olives can also added.

Vegetable Quiche

Ingredients.....................Quantity

Dough...3 ½ oz (100 g)

Butter..2 oz (60 g)

Sugar...2 tbsp

Salt ....½ tbsp

Oregano ....¼ tbsp

Chilled Water..................................10-15 ml

For filling

Mixed Vegetables -
(Carrot, Beans, Capsicum).................... 1 cup

Parsley ....¼ tbsp

Tomato Puree...................................¼ tbsp

Pizza Chesse.............................3 ½ oz (100 g)

White Sauce

Flour..1 tsp

Butter...½ cup

Milk..1 cup

Oregano..¼ tsp

Parsley..¼ tbsp

Salt..2 pinches

White Pepper...¼ tbsp

Preparation

1. Sieve the flour with the sugar and salt. Mix the butter to this flour mix with the help of your fingers. Do not knead the dough.

2. Sprinkle the milk which should be chilled on the flour and collect it in a plastic bag.

3. Refrigerate the dough for about 15 minutes

4. Roll the dough and cut it into rounds and these rounds need not be greased.

5. Trim the excess of dough from the corners. Prick it all over with the help of a fork.

6. Pre heat the Air Fryer at 140*C (285*F) for about 5 minutes. Arrange it in the fry basket for 15-20 minutes at 140*C (285*F).

7. Let it cook until it turns golden. Remove them from the pastry shells. Cool them down under room temperature.

8. Now for the quiche, fry the onions till they turn brown. Add all the other vegetables like capsicum. Add the tomato puree now. Saute this mixture for another 5-6 minutes.

9. Add required amount of salt and pepper.

To Prepare the White Sauce :

10.   Heat butter in a pan and add maida. Keep stirring for a minute or so till it turns frothy.

11. Add milk to this mixture. Add sugar to this mixture. Add salt and pepper to this. Mix some cheese in the mix.

12. Make a layer with the vegetables and garnish with olives.

13. Cook this in the Air fryer at 160*C (320*F) for about 10 minutes.

Extra Facts

Serve hot with tomato ketchup.

Chapter 3

Snacks

Table of Contents

Cream Samosa

Ingredients....................Quantity

For the pastry Skin

Thick Cream ....250 ml
Flour ....2 cups
Salt...½ tsp
Black Pepper...¼ tsp
Cumin ....¼ tsp

For the Filling

Butter...4 tbsp
Onion (Chopped).....................................1
Garlic (Minced)......................................2-3 tsp
Ginger (Minced).....................................1 tsp
Potato (Peeled into cubes)....................1

Carrot (Peeled)....................................2-3

Peas..1 cup

Salt..2 tsp

Black Pepper....................................¼ tsp

Chillies..¼ tsp

Corn Oil..2 tsp

Preparation

1. Mix the cream, flour, salt, pepper and cumin and place it as a dough mix and knead it for about 2 to 4 minutes.

2. Wrap the dough in a plastic cling wrap and let it be cold for about half an hour.

3. The pastry skin is brought to room temperature and is rolled into balls of 1-inch diameter, cut the edges and make the pastry into triangles of desired samosa sizes.

4. Meanwhile, Fry onion, ginger, garlic with butter, add potatoes, carrot, peas, spices with salt and pepper.

5. Simmer for about 10 minutes. Let the vegetable boil and not get soggy. Now stuff the vegetables over the pastry skin.

6. Fill the skin with the vegetable stuffing and fry it in the air fryer at 220*C (430*F).

7. Serve the samosas with tomato ketchup.

Extra Facts

Instead of the vegetables, the stuffing can also be fried meat and can be made as chicken or mutton Keema samosa.

Meat Sandwich with Tomato Paste

Ingredients......................Quantity

Corn Oil..2 tbsp

Onion (Minced, Large).......................1

 Meat (Minced)...........................10 oz (300 g)

Cloves...2

Garlic..2

Cumin ....1 tsp

Sugar..1 tsp

Tomato Paste.....................................1 packet

Water...¼ cup

Salt...1 tsp

Sandwich Burger................................4

Preparation

1. Heat oil, saute the onions, garlic and ginger under low flame.

2. Add the meat to the mixture and fry for about 5 minutes.

3. Add chilli, cumin, sugar, tomato paste and black pepper and cook for 15 minutes.

4. Place the paste in between the sandwich burger pieces and bake for 3 minutes in the Air Fryer at 180*C (355*F).

Extra Facts

One can also add cheese to the burger sandwich slices.

We can also include other vegetables of our liking to the filling.

Veg Fritters/ The Indian Pakoda

Ingredients....................Quantity

Gram Flour...Half Cup

Salt...2 tsp

Turmeric Powder...............................½ tsp

Red Chilli Powder.............................1 tsp

Cumin Powder....................................½ tsp

Veggies (of your choice).....................2-3

Preparation

1. The batter is prepared by mixing flour, salt, turmeric powder, red chilli powder and cumin powder with required amount of water.

2. Make sure the mix does not get too watery.

3. Soak the veggies in the batter till the veggies are fully covered with the batter.

4. The fritters are then placed on a butter paper and brushed with required amount of oil.

5. The Air Fryer is pre heated at 200*C (390*F) for about 3 minutes and is left to cook for 10 minutes.

Extra Facts

The veggies can also be replaced with boiled eggs and egg fritters can be made the same way.

Tissue paper can be used to dry out the excess oil in case of oil conscious people.

French Fries with Meat Sauce

Ingredients.....................Quantity

Onion (Minced, Large) 1

Garlic, Cloves (Minced)........................1

Corn Oil..2 tbsp

Meat (Minced)...............................7 oz (200 g)

Tomato (Large, Peeled and Minced)....2

Salt...1 tsp

Black Pepper...1 tsp

Corriander (Dried)..................................1 tsp

Potato Fingers (Fried)......................4 packets

Cheese (Shredded)...............................½ cup

Preparation

1. Heat oil, add onion, garlic and pepper. Mix the meat and let the mixture dry.

2. Add the tomatoes with the salt, cumin and coriander, cook on low heat for 10 minutes.

3. Place the potato fingers in a plate, sprinkle cheese in abundance or less as required. Add the meat mix to the fries

and leave it in the Air Fryer for 5 minutes at 180*C (355*F).

Extra Facts

Serve the French fries with spicy pickles to match the meat.

Stuffed Potatoes

Ingredients.....................Quantity

Gram Flour ....3 tbsp

Onions (Large, Chopped)......................1

Coconut (Freshly grated)......................2 tbsp

Turmeric Powder...................................½ tbsp

Cumin Powder..½ tbsp

Salt...2 tbsp

Potatoes...6-8

Preparation

1. In a bowl, mix the gram flour with the chopped onions, coconut, turmeric powder, red chilli powder, cumin powder and salt.

2. These mix to form a masala for the stuffing purpose.

3. Coat the veggies with the masala and let it set for 10 minutes.

4. Pre heat the Air Fryer at 200*C (390*F) for 3 minutes and put the vegetables in the frying basket and let them cook for 10 minutes.

Extra Facts

The recipe can also be used with other vegetables like ladies finger.

Prawn Cutlet

Ingredients.....................Quantity

Minced Prawns ....½ cup

Breadcrumps.......................................½ cup

Onions (Medium, Chopped)...............1 cup

Ginger- Garlic Paste...........................1 tsp

Turmeric Powder.................................½ tsp

Red Chilli Powder..............................½ tsp

Salt..2 tsp

Preparation

1. In a bowl mix all the ingredients with the prawns. Add required amount of salt.

2. Mix them together and make cutlets. Dust them with any flour of your choice.

3. Pre heat the Air Fryer for 200*C (390*F) for 3 minutes and cook the cutlets for about 5-6 minutes.

Extra Facts

Add some chopped veggies with the cutlet and serve them hot.

We can also serve the cutlets with mayonnaise.

Chicken Momos

Ingredients....................Quantity

Dough

Maida....................................1 cup

Salt ....½ tsp

Water...................................½ cup

Filling

Chicken (Minced)....................1 cup

Cabbage (Grated)....................1 cup

Capsicum...............................½ cup

Ginger-Garlic Paste................1 tbsp

Soya Sauce............................1 tsp

Vinegar................................½ tsp

Preparation

1. Knead the flour and salt together with water to make it semi greasy. Cover the dough with little drops of oil. Let it set for 10 to 15 minutes.

2. Heat oil in a pan and add the ginger garlic paste with onions. Wait till the onions turn brown.

3. Add the minced chicken to the onions. Saute them for 2 to 3 minutes. Add the cabbage and capsicum to this.

4. Add soya sauce, salt and vinegar to this mixture. Let it cool for a while.

5. Roll the dough and place the filling in the centre.

6. Pre heat the Air Fryer for 5 minutes at 140*C (285*F). Let the momos cook for about 20-25 minutes.

Extra Facts

We can serve the momos with chilli sauce or green chutney.

Chilli Paneer

Ingredients.....................Quantity

Cottage Cheese...........................5 oz (150 g)

Capsicum (Big, cut into cubes).............1

Red Onion (Small)...............................1

Spring Onion...1

Marinate

Ginger-Garlic Paste..................................1 tbsp

Red chilli sauce...1 tbsp

Salt..2 tsp

Pepper...2 tsp

Coating

Corn Flour...3 tbsp

Gravy

Green chillies (Finely Chopped)………1-2 nos

Ginger…………………………………………½ tsp

Garlic (Chopped)………………………………1 tsp

Tomato Ketchup………………………………3 tbsp

Vinegar………………………………………2 tsp

Soya Sauce……………………………………2 tsp

Water…………………………………………1 cup

Olive Oil………………………………………1 tbsp

Preparation

1. Cut the cottage cheese pieces so that they remain attached to one another.

2. Mix the marinade ingredients together and make it as a paste. Apply the

marinade paste uniformly over the cottage cheese.

3. Roll the cheese with the corn flour.

4. Pre heat the Air Fryer for 5 minutes at 180*C (355*F).

5. Cook the pieces for 20 minutes at the same temperature about another 20 minutes. Turn the pieces as they cook so that they are fried uniformly.

6. Prepare the gravy by heating the olive oil with garlic, green chillies and ginger. Add some onions and saute them for 2 minutes. Cook this with the ginger garlic paste and fry till the mixture is softened by cooking.

7. Add the sauce mixture and let the mixture boil for some time. The water and corn flour mix is then added to it.

8. Add cheese and green onions. Cook them and the sauce is left to settle over the cottage cheese.

Extra Facts

The Cottage Cheese can be served with green chutney.

Cornflakes French Toast

Ingredients.....................Quantity

Brown Bread Slices...............................2

Egg (White)...1

Sugar (Crushed)......................................2 tsp

Cornflakes (Crushed)............................2 cups

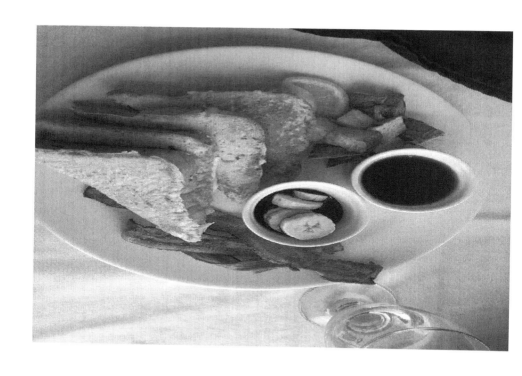

Preparation

1. Cut the bread into triangles.

2. Whisk the egg whites with the sugar and beat them to form a homogenous mixture.

3. Dip the bread into the mixture and with the sugar mixture.

4. Coat the bread with the dry corn flakes.

5. Pre heat the Air Fryer at 180*C (355*F) for about 5 minutes.

6. Arrange the breads in the fry basket. Let the bread bake for about 15 to 20 minutes at 180*C (355*F).

7. Let the breads cool down at room temperature.

Extra Facts

Serve the breads with chocolate sauce.

Mathri

Ingredients.....................Quantity

Ghee ....1 oz (25 g)

Flour..1 cup

Salt...To taste

Ajwain..½ tbsp

Jeera...½ tsp

Preparation

1. Sieve the flour and add the salt with the jeera. The jeera has to be roasted in oil or ghee.

2. Mix it well and water has to be collected so that a dough is formed.

3. The dough is made into balls of a lemon size and is pressed between the palms.

4. Pre heat the Air Fryer for about 5 minutes at 140*C (285*F). the Mathri is cooked at 180*C (355*F) for about 15 minutes.

5. Arrange the Mathri in a fry basket and let it bake for some time.

6. Keep turning the Mathri so that it is cooked uniformly.

7. The Mathri is let it cool down.

Extra Facts

It is stored in an air tight container.

Barbeque Corn Sandwich

Ingredients....................Quantity

White Bread..4 slices

Butter (Softened)...............................2 tbsp

Sweet Corn Kernels............................1 cup

Capsicum (Small)................................1

Barbeque Sauce..................................1 tsp

Olive Oil..1 tsp

Onion (Chopped)...............................½ cup

Garlic (Crushed)................................1 flake

Mustard Powder.................................¼ tsp

Sugar...½ tbsp

Tomato Ketchup.................................½ tbsp

Red Chilli Sauce.................................½ tbsp

Water...½ cup

Salt...To taste

Pepper...To taste

Preparation

1. Slice the edges of the breads and cut them horizontally.

2. In a pan, fry onions and garlic with oil and let them cook for 4 minutes till they turn soft. Add the mustard, sugar and chilli sauce. We can add water to the mixture.

3. Let the mixture boil and reduce the flame. Let the mixture simmer for about 8 to 10 minutes. This is done till the sauce reduces and thickens to some extent.

4. In a pan, add butter and roast the corn kernels till the dark spots appear on the corn.

5. Roast the capsicum and let it cook completely. The black skin is then peeled off and chopped finely.

6. Mix corn and the capsicum in a bowl and spread the mixture on the bread.

7. Now place the second bread over the first bread and pre heat the air fryer at 180*C (355*F) for 5 minutes.

8. Arrange the sandwich in the fry basket and let it fry.

9. Let the sandwich cook for 15 minutes at 180*C (355*F).

10. Repeat the same procedure with other slices of bread.

Extra Facts

Serve the sandwiches with chocolate sauce or tomato ketchup.

Cheesy Vegetable Wrap

Ingredients.....................Quantity

Flour ....2 cups
Baking Powder......................................½ tsp
Salt...¼ tsp
Oil..4 tbsp
Water...As Required

Filling

Carrots (Finely Chopped).......................½ cup
Beans (Finely Chopped).........................12 nos
Cabbage ....½ cup
Capsicum (Chopped into cubes)..............½ cup
Onions (Finely Chopped).........................2
Olive oil..2 tsp
Tomato Ketchup....................................3 tbsp

Oregano..¼ tbsp

Basil..¼ tbsp

Parsley...¼ tbsp

Salt and Pepper..............................To Taste

Cheese (Grated)...............................4 tbsp

Sealing

Flour...1 tbsp

Water.......................................to make paste

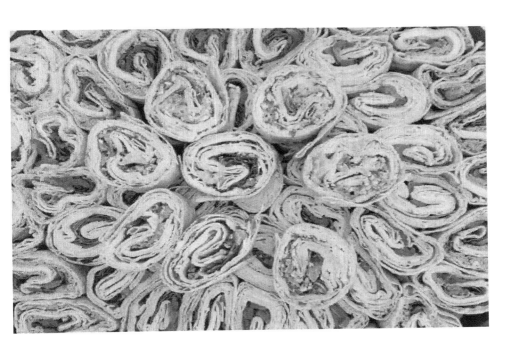

Preparation

1. Partially boil all the vegetables. Capsicum should be left out.

2. Strain the water.

3. Take oil in a pan. Saute the onions till they become golden brown. Now, add all the vegetables with the capsicum cubes and let it saute for 6 minutes.

4. Add the seasonings to the veggies and the tomato puree to this mixture.

5. Add a little salt and pepper to this mixture. Let the filling cool down.

6. Sieve the flour and the baking powder together. Add salt and the oil till we get a bread crump like consistency with the mixture.

7. Knead this using water or milk in case we need a softer dough.

8. Make about 5 to 6 balls from the dough and roll them into the shape of chapattis with 6-7 inches diameter.

9. In a tawa, cook both the sides of the roti.

10. Ensure that the roti does not have any black spots while cooking.

11. Fill the roti with the filling. Spread some cheese and fold the roti from all the sides. Make this a rectangular wrap.

12. Seal the roll using flour and paste at all the edges.

13. Pre heat the Air Fryer at 180*C (355*F) for 5 minutes. Arrange the rolls in the fry basket and let it cook.

14. Let the rolls cook uniformly at 180*C (355*F) for 15 minutes.

Extra Facts

The rolls can be served with ketchup.

Aloo Bondas

Ingredients..................Quantity

Potatoes

(Big, Boiled and Mashed).................. 2

Garam Masala Powder......................¼ tsp

Ginger (Finely Chopped).................... ½ tsp

Green Chilli (Finely Chopped)........... ½ cup

Lemon Juice....................................½ tbsp

Coriander Leaves..............................½ tsp

Red Chilli Powder............................½ tbsp

Saunf Powder....................................1 tsp

Besan Batter

Besan..1 cup

Salt and Red Chilli Powder...................to taste

Water ....to make batter

...........................Coating

Corn Flakes...................................Crushed

Salt and Chilli powde.....................To taste

Preparation

1. Add ginger, green chillies, coriander leaves and curry leaves with the masalas.

2. The mixture is applied to the potatoes. Mix them well.

3. Make round balls of small lemon size.

4. With the besan batter dip the potatoes and then coat them with the cornflakes.

5. Repeat the same procedure with other round balls also.

6. Pre heat the Air Fryer at 160*C (320*F) for 5 minutes.

7. Cook them for about 20 minutes at the same temperature.

Extra Facts

Serve them hot with ketchup or mayonnaise.

Chapter 4

Desserts

Table of Contents

Oreo Biscuit Cake

Ingredients.....................Quantity

Oreo Biscuits.......................................10-12

Milk...1 cup

Baking Soda..½ tsp

Baking Powder....................................1 tsp

Slivered Almonds................................1 tbsp

Dry Fruits.......................................To Garnish

Preparation

1. Grind the biscuits to get the fine consistency for the cake.

2. Mix Milk, Baking Soda, Baking Powder, Silvered Almonds in a bowl. Please ensure that no lumps are formed in this process.

3. The Air Fryer should be greased with oil and pour the batter into it. Let the batter settle inside properly.

4. Optional: Sprinkle the dry fruits over the batter for rich taste.

5. Pre heat the air fryer at 200* C (390*F) for about 3 minutes and let the pan stay for another 8 minutes.

6. One can add cream over the cake to make it all the more desirable.

Extra Facts

As the cake involves no butter or any cholesterol related ingredients, it is absolutely fat-free.

Vanilla Cookies

Ingredients......................Quantity

Gram Flour ....½ cup

Semolina...1 cup

Flour (Maida)......................................1 cup

Ghee..1 tbsp

Powdered Sugar.................................1 cup

Vanilla Essence..................................1 tsp

Pistachios ....To Garnish

Preparation

1. Mix the gram flour, semolina and flour (Maida) in a bowl.

2. Add few drops of ghee to the mixture of flour. Add vanilla essence and powdered sugar to the flour mix.

3. Knead this mix into a dough and make it in the shape of cookie biscuits.

4. Over the dough, place the pistachios and bake them in the airfryer.

5. Preheat the airfryer for 3 minutes at 180*C (355*F) and bake the cookies till they turn brown in color.

Extra Facts

One can add other flavours of essence for different types of cookies.

Red Velvet Cup Cakes

Ingredients.....................Quantity

Flour.....................................1/3 cups

Baking Soda...........................½ tsp

Baking Powder......................½ tsp

Salt..¼ tsp

Castor...................................1 cup

Butter..................................¼ cup

Vanilla Essence....................1 tsp

Unsweetened Cocoa..............1 tbsp

Raspberry syrup...................1 tbsp

Buttermilk............................¼ cup

Garnishing

Whipping Cream...................1 cup

Icing sugar...........................1 tbsp

Vanilla Essence.......................................½ tbsp

Preparation

1. Line up 5 to 6 cups of muffin .

2. In a bowl sieve the flour with baking soda , baking powder and salt together.

3. Beat the butter with the sugar and add vanilla essence to this mixture.

4. The cocoa powder is then added to the butter and combined at a slower pace.

5. After half an hour add the buttermilk and the flour to the mixture.

6. Beat them up so that no lumps were formed.

7. Spread the batter over the muffins and prepare them according to the serving demand.

8. Pre heat the Air Fryer for 25 minutes at 140*C (285*F).

9. With the help of a toothpick we can keep the cup cake clean when it is baked. Add the whipping cream with vanilla essence and top this with icing sugar.

Extra Facts

We can cool the cupcakes down to enhance the taste and the flavours.

Chocolate Tarts

Ingredients.....................Quantity

Flour...3 oz (90 g)

Cocoa Powder..............................1/3 oz (10 g)

Nutralite..2 oz (60 g)

Powdered Sugar.............................1 oz (30 g)

Chilled Milk/Water...........................10-15 ml

Filling

Chopped Chocolate....................4 ½ oz (125 g)

Cream..1 ¾ oz (50 g)

Butter...2 tbsp

Cashew Slices.......................................½ cup

Preparation

1. Sieve the sugar with the flour.

2. The flour mixture is mixed with sugar as it appears like bread crumps.

3. Sprinkle a small amount of chilled milk over the flour mixture and not knead the dough.

4. Cover this mix with a plastic bag.

5. Refrigerate this mix for about half an hour.

6. Roll the dough and cut them into pieces of shapes of your choice.

7. Trim the excess dough with the help of a pin. Prick it all over with a fork.

8. Pre heat the Air Fryer for about 5 minutes at 140*C (285*F). Fry the mix for 15 to 20 minutes at the same temperature.

9. Remove from the fryer and let it cool. Fill in with truffle fillings. Sprinkle over the cashew slices.

Extra Facts

The sprinkling over can be any nuts of your choice. Plums can also be used.

Eggless Chocolate Sponge Cake

Ingredients.....................Quantity

Milk Maid..½ cup

Flour...2 cups

Cocoa Powder...¼ cup

Baking Soda..¼ tsp

Oil..½ cup

Sugar (Powdered)..................................2 tbsp

Soda..¼ cup

Vanilla Essence......................................½ cup

Butter Paper..1

Preparation

1. The maida is mixed with cocoa, baking soda and baking powder. Keep it aside.

2. Beat the milk maid for about 5 minutes until it turns fluffy and white in color.

3. Add sugar to the milk maid and beat it for another 10 minutes.

4. Add oil to this mixture. Beat well till the mixture becomes uniform in consistency.

5. Now soda is added between rounds. Beat till you attain the ribbon consistency.

6. The mixture is poured into the greased tin and put into the Air Fryer.

7. The Air Fryer is pre heated for 5 minutes at 140*C (285*F). Keep the tin in the frying basket and maintain the temperature. Let it bake for about 20 minutes.

8. De mould the cake and let it cool for sometime.

9. Store the cake in a refrigerator.

Extra Facts

Garnish with nuts and refrigerate.

Eggless Brownies

Ingredients......................Quantity

Butter..2 oz (60 g)

Water..1 tbsp

Nuts (Chopped)....................................¼ cup

Melted Chocolat........................3 ½ oz (100 g)

Flour..1 tbsp

Milk Maid...½ cup

Preparation

1. Sieve the flour with nuts and keep it aside.

2. Melt the chocolate and the butter in a microwave for 30 seconds.

3. Keep stirring the molten chocolate for sometime. Let the chocolate melt completely.

4. Add milk maid to this mixture.

5. Pre heat the Air Fryer for about 5 minutes at 140*C (285*F).

6. Keep the fryer running for 30 minutes with the mixture.

7. Mould the brownies and transfer them to plates as they cool down.

8. Let it cool down for 45 minutes before they are cut into pieces.

Extra Facts

The brownies can be served with chocolate sauce or with vanilla ice cream.

Custard Cookies

Ingredients......................Quantity

Flour..½ oz (75 g)

Icing Sugar...½ cup

Custard Powder............................2 ½ oz (75 g)

Nutralite...1 pinch

Baking Soda.................................1 ¾ oz (50 g)

Baking Powder............................1 ¾ oz (50 g)

Preparation

1. Cream the margarine using an electric beater.

2. Mix the sugar powder in the magarine and apply cream to spread the sugar uniformly.

3. Sieve the flour, custard powder, baking powder and soda together.

4. The cream is then mixed with the flour mixture.

5. Do not knead the flour but spread it even.

6. Roll the dough into balls and coat it with the dry dough further.

7. Pre heat the Air Fryer at 140*C (285*F) for about 5 minutes.

8. Fry the mixture at the same temperature for 15 to 20 minutes till they turn golden in colour.

9. Let it cool for about 20 minutes.

Extra Facts

Do not knead the flour but mix it with hands.

Honey Chilli Potatoes

Ingredients....................Quantity

Potato Fingers (Peeled, Washed)....... 2

Cold Water.......................................2 cups

Ginger Garlic Paste............................2 tsp

Red Chilli Sauce.................................1 tsp

Salt...¼ tsp

Red Chilli Powder...............................¼ tsp

Sauce

Olive Oil..1 tbsp

Capsicum (Cut, Long Strips)..................1

Onions (Small, Half rings).....................2

Ginger Garlic Paste...............................1 tsp

Tomato Ketchup................................2 tbsp

Vinegar ....2 tsp

Soya Sauce..2 tsp

Black Pepper Powder............................½ tsp

Spring Onions.................................To Garnish

Preparation

1. In a small bowl, mix the ginger garlic paste, red chilli sauce and the salt together.

2. Dry the potatoes in a towel.

3. Mix the Potatoes with the paste prepared above. Mix the coat.

4. Pre heat the air fryer at 160*C (320*F) for 5 minutes. Arrange the potatoes in the fry basket and close it.

5. Cook the potatoes at 160*C (320*F) for about 30 minutes.

6. For the Sauce:

7. Mix the ketchup, red chilli sauce, soya sauce and the pepper powder. Mix well.

8. Add onions which are sauted separately to this mixture. Add the ginger garlic paste to this. Cook this until it looks crunchy.

9. Mix all the sauces, chilli flakes and pepper. Add the air fried potatoes to this sauce. Add the sauce to the potatoes and let it cool down for a while.

Extra Facts

This can be served as a starter also.

Conclusion

The idea behind the making of this book is to provide you the reader with a variety of recipes to choose from to be cooked using your airfryer. The airfryer is a revolutionary kitchen appliance in the frying and cooking of food and to be able to prepare healthy delicious meals is what I looked to provide in this book. I do not believe that healthy cooking and eating should be a restriction but rather an area to explore excessively and the airfryer allows for just that.

I hope that the recipes presented in this book will allow you to create amazingly delicious meals and that you will continue to use your airfryer to satisfy those cravings for fried foods but in a healthy way.

As you've come to the end of this book I would like to thank you for reading through and I do wish that you use this book to prepare mouth watering meals.

Made in the USA
Lexington, KY
02 August 2016